INTRODUCTION

The Indian ring-necked parakeet, also called the rose-winged parakeet, has been kept as a pet for centuries and remains a favorite companion bird today. A devoted owner will do best with this temperamental bird that requires a great deal of attention to remain tame. However, the Indian ring-necked will charm and delight the person who takes the time to appreciate its other qualities — a playful exuberance and a remarkable talking ability.

Indian ring-necked parakeets are sensitive birds that need lots of play time and time out of the cage to remain happy; if not, expect your bird to develop neurotic disorders that many be very difficult to reverse.

Because of the long tail, Indian ring necks need a larger cage than another bird of the same relative size. Ring necks love their toys, and will hang on them and toss them around the cage, so be sure to have lots of toys on hand to replace the ones your bird destroys — this type of destruction is a normal, healthy part of being a companion bird. If you can handle a good deal of chattering, some of it ear-piercing, and you have the time and energy to spend with this beautiful bird, consider welcoming an Indian ring-necked parakeet into your family.A captive bred Indian Ringneck Parakeet can range in coloring. Blues, yellows, albinos and greens are common colorations and these variants in color have made them extremely popular as pets. In captivity, they are able to live approximately twenty-five to thirty years, although some have been known to live longer. Taking on an Indian Ringneck Parakeet as a pet, can be a very rewarding experience but owners need to realize that there is responsibility involved. Their diets in the wild do not only consist of seeds, so owners will have to throw in a few fruits and vegetables to ensure that they get a balanced diet. Food and water bowls should also be cleaned every day, as dirty bowls pose a danger for infections and bacteria growth. Their high intelligence gives them the ability to talk, perform tricks and mimic human behavior, but it also means that they can get very bored, very quickly. Owners should shower them with as much attention as possible and ensure that their cages always have toys for them to play with. Ropes and knots seem to be very effective as they enjoy the challenge of loosening the knot and climbing the ropes.

Indian Ringneck Parakeets are known to be very affectionate and gentle companions, with most owners finding that the males are generally gentler, than the females. But with enough love and attention, both male and females are wonderful feathered friends that will gladly accept a scratch or a cuddle.

ORIGIN AND HISTORY

The Indian ringneck parakeet is an Asiatic subspecies of the rose-ringed parakeet (Psittacula krameri). It is an Asiatic parrot originally from Ceylon. Now, you can find it in many parts of Asia, notably India and Pakistan. It also lives in the western and southern areas of Sudan and the Middle East.

In the wild, they live in lightly timbered areas, as well as farmed areas of the countryside. They travel in flocks of 100 or more birds, so they are used to having company.

Indian ringneck parakeets have been kept in captivity from as early as 200 BC. In India, they were regarded as sacred beings after religious leaders began to recognize their ability to mimic human language clearly. Highly regarded by wealthy Indian royals, ringneck parrots were kept in decorative cages and admired for their colors and charming dispositions.

During the 1920s, aviculturists began breeding captive ringnecks, and, with the advent of different color mutations, the popularity of the bird started to explode. Now widely available in the pet trade, Indian ringneck parakeets continue to gain increasing popularity as pets. Their relatively small size and beautiful markings help to make the ringneck the right choice for many bird owners.

PHYSICAL DESCRIPTION

Psittacula krameri is a medium sized bird with a body length on average of about 38.1 cm long; however, this number can range from 38-42 cm. It has a body mass of about 137.0 g. These birds have a green body with a reddish beak. They have a rather long pointed tail that is more than half of the body's length. This tail can be up to 25 cm long. The males of this species show a dark purplish color around their necks, giving the ring-necked parakeet its name. The young birds do not show this coloring on their necks, however. They only acquire it once they reach sexual maturity which is about the age of three. The female birds do not have this rose colored ring around their necks. At hatching, the young are altricial meaning they are rather undeveloped and require care from their parents.

DISTRIBUTION/RANGE

Indian Ringnecks originated in Sri Lanka. Their extensive native range now includes Pamban or Rameswaram Island (an island located between India and Sri Lanka), the Indian sub-continent, Pakistan, Afghanistan, Nepal, as well as the Burmese region to Cochinchina (the southern third of Vietnam. They are common throughout most of their natural range

Introduced (feral) populations exist worldwide:

United States: Florida, California and Hawaii

South America

Europe:

United Kingdom - the largest numbers are found around south London, with populations occurring in or around Battersea Park, Richmond Park, and Hampstead Heath. Smaller flocks occur in Esher (South East England in the Greater London Urban Area), and Berkshire (South England); as well as Margate, Broadstairs and Ramsgate, Kent. Small groups are occasionally seen in Dorset, Kensington Gardens (London), South Manchester and Studland).

Belgium, Spain, Canary Islands, etc.

Netherlands: Amsterdam, Rotterdam, Utrecht and The Hague

Belgium: Brussels

Germany: Occur along the Rhine in major urban areas, such as Cologne, Bonn, Ludwigshafen, and Heidelberg and Wiesbaden. Also in northeastern Hamburg

France: Around Paris

Italy: Rome (in the gardens of the Palatine Hill and at Villa Borghese)

Spain: Barcelona

Blue Mutation Indian RIngneck ParakeetAfrica: Tunis - the capital of Tunisia (the northernmost country in Africa); South Africa

Middle East: Iran (mostly in northern Tehran); Lebanon, Israel, United Arab Emirates (UAE), Bahrain, Qatar, and Oman

Japan: Hundreds of escaped pets established themselves in southwestern Tokyo, Chiba, Kanagawa, Aichi, Kyoto, Hiroshima Prefecture, Niigata, Tochigi, Saitama, Shizuoka, Gifu, Osaka, Ehime, Saga and Miyazaki Prefecture

Australia

AVICULTURE

Ringnecks are unsuitable as "starter birds," and should not be placed in mixed species collections due to aggressive tendencies. Although they are being kept successfully with larger species in spacious aviaries.

The aviary construction should be a steel frame with heavy duty wire netting (i.e., 16g welded mesh). As they like to chew, wood construction is unsuitable for them. For adjacent flights, double wired partitions are needed, as they will attack those that hang on to the wide of the aviary, causing damage to their feet and beaks. For better breeding results, consider visual barriers.

Ringnecks are active birds that do best in large flights or aviaries that allow them to fly and exercise. A good size flight would be 10'x 10' x 15' (3 x 3 x 5 meters). The minimum length of a flight should be 7 feet (2 meters).

They need a suitable sheltered area that protects them from draft, cold weather and rain. In warmer areas, this can be achieved by covering part of the aviary (both the sides and the roof) with clear or opaque corrugated roofing material. The rest should be kept open to give access to sun and rain. Those kept in colder climates may need a heated sheltered area as they are susceptible to chilling and frost bitten toes.

Non-toxic leafy branches make excellent perches and should be placed at both ends of the flight for them to chew and perch on. The Ringnecks will chew any leaves, flowers and fruiting bodies off, as well as gnaw on the wood, which provides entertainment and good beak exercise. These branches will need to be replaced regularly.

If the birds are kept in a communal / aviary setting, it is best to separate breeding pairs for the breeding season, as they will be more aggressive during this time. Best results are achieved if each breeding pair has its own flight, ensuring that the pairs can't see each other. As these birds don't form strong pair bonds, they may "flirt" with birds in other aviaries which could potentially interfere with breeding successes for both pairs. This being said, it is possible to keep two pairs in a large flight - however, both pairs need to be introduced into the flight at the same time to prevent territorial aggression.

Ringnecks usually only raise one brood a season - although if one clutch is removed for artificial incubation or lost for whatever reason, the female will usually lay another clutch to replace the previous one. In warmer areas of the world (such as southern USA, South Africa and Austalia), they regularly produce two clutches.

It is important to discourage breeding when temperatures are still chilly as this increases the chance of problems, such as egg binding, chilled eggs or chicks, or dead or crippled chicks. Breeders may remove the nesting boxes or seal the entrance holes to the boxes until weather warms up to discourage early nesting.

It is best to provide two nesting boxes for each pair to choose from. The nesting birds may show a preference for a nest box of the type and size they themselves were hatched and raised in. If this information is not available, providing nestboxes or logs of various sizes and types, and placed in various locations within the aviary, may make it easier for the parents to make their choice.

The nest box should be situated in a sheltered part of the flight, about 5 - 6 feet (1.5 - 1.8 meters) above the ground. It is important, however, to not place the nest box too close to the roof as this could result in heat problems during the summer. Once a pair has chosen their favorite nest box, it should be kept for their exclusive use. Any others can be removed at this point. At the end of the breeding season, their nest box should be thoroughly cleaned and sanitized.

Nest box options / considerations:

Solid, deep log - often preferred by wild-caught birds that were raised in natural tree cavities. The recommended size is about 8 - 10 inches (~200 - 250 mm)

Nestbox: About 7 - 10" wide x 7 - 10" deep x 18 - 30" high. As these parrots are heavy chewers, the box should be made of a thick timber or 3/4-1 inch thick exterior quality plywood. Depending on the depth of the nest box may require a climbing structure inside the box just below the entrance hole. The nest box should have a removable top / lid to facilitate nest inspections.

Entrance hole: Can be either square or round, with a diameter of about 3 inches (75 mm) diameter. The entrance should be about 4 - 6 inches (~100 -150 mm) from the top.

Suitable nesting material should cover the bottom of the nest box, such as soft sieved sand, safe (non-toxic) saw dust, pine or wood shavings, dried plant material or other suitable materials.

A clutch may consist of 3 to 5 white eggs. In some instances, only 2 are laid, or as many as 6 eggs. The eggs are laid one every other day. The incubation may not start until two or more of the eggs have been laid. The incubation usually lasts between 21 - 24 days. The female incubates the eggs alone, while the male feeds the brooding female. The hatchlings are blind and naked, and depend on their parents for warmth and feeding.

Male Indian Ringneck (Normal Green)The parents will need to be provided with plenty of food to allow them to feed their growing, hungry chicks.

These parrots generally tolerate nest inspections quite well, and the nests should be inspected daily to ensure the wellbeing of the chicks.

Once the chicks are 7 - 10 days old, breeders will generally place closed metal leg rings on one of the chicks' legs for accurate record keeping or as proof of captive-bred stock, in areas where this is required.

Those chicks destined for the pet market should be well socialized to ensure tameness and good pet qualities.

The young usually fledge when they are about 6 - 8 weeks old, but they still depend on their parents for another 3 - 4 weeks. They can be left with their parents for 6 months or longer. As the parents get ready for their next breeding session, aggression towards their previous young may occur, at which time they will need to be removed.

BREEDING INDIAN RINGNECKS

Breeding Indian Ringnecks is not difficult, but does require the birds have some privacy. Ringnecks can breed once a year nd will not breed year round like some parrot species. These birds prefer to breed during the spring and molt during the hotter seasons.

These birds are often housed in large aviaries and separated in pairs during the breeding season. These birds cannot be housed together as the female is very aggressive and will kill any intruders that enter her territory.

When breeding season approaches, place a deep nesting box inside the aviary. Once the female is ready to start breeding, she will spend countless hours inside her box scratching around for materials to build their nest. Most breeders place wood shavings in the bottom of the nesting box before the breeding season begins. Many females will remove this layer of shaving, but if this should happen, the breeder should simply refill the nesting box.

Ringnecks become very affectionate when in breeding mode. Usually, most Indian Ringnecks avoid affectionate behavior when placed with other birds, but when breeding, they start to preen and feed each other. When this behavior is observed, eggs can be expected about two weeks later.

Female ringnecks lay between three and six white eggs; one egg every other day. The female will start incubating the eggs as soon as the second or third egg is laid. The incubation period lasts 23 days, and the chicks will make a small hole from inside the eggs before they hatching. Once hatched, the babies will stay with the mother until they are at least 10 weeks old or weaned.

If the owner wishes to hand feed the babies, they should be pulled when the oldest chick is about 15 days old.

When weaning baby ringnecks, the owner can expect their babies to wean around 10-14 weeks. Ringnecks that are kept alone take much longer to wean than if kept with their parents. This is normal and the breeder should never starve the bird to encourage weaning. In fact, feeding more throughout the day as the bird matures stimulates the bird to eat solid foods instead of begging for food all day.

GENERAL DESCRIPTION

Indian ringneck parakeets range between 14 and 17 inches long; approximately half of their body length comes from their long tail feathers. They get their name from the thin black chinstrap that wraps around the necks of males. In the wild, these medium-sized parrots are most typically bright green with accents of yellow or bluish-gray, but captive parakeets come in more than 30 different color varieties as the result of breeding. Young ringnecks look very similar to their parents, although their colors are less brilliant than those of adults.

BREEDING SEASON

In the wild, these colorful parrots typically breed between February and March, although this season is slightly extended in some cases. In introduced areas, however, the breeding season will vary depending on the climate. For example, Joyce Baum, a seasoned ringneck breeder who lives in Arizona, mentions in one of her articles that her ringnecks typically start working their nest box in December. The breeding season doesn't only encompass the physical act of breeding, but also courting, finding a suitable mate and choosing a suitable nesting cavity.

NESTING CAVITIES

Indian ringnecks prefer the opportunistic approach to finding a nesting cavity. Old holes previously excavated by woodpeckers or barbets work well for these medium-sized birds. Holes in the walls of a building also will work for these opportunistic nesters. The ideal cavity entrance should be typically around 2 inches or more. If they don't find a proper cavity or nest box, ringnecks will excavate their own using their powerful beaks and claws.

EGG LAYING

Females typically lay an average clutch of between two and six small, whitish eggs. For the three weeks after laying, she incubates her eggs. Once the young hatch, both father and mother take turns caring for their young. According to the Royal Society for the Protection of Birds, Indian ringnecks experience high nesting success. The young fledge when they are between 40 and 50 days old; they're sexually mature between 1 and 1 1/2 years old.

REPRODUCTION

The rose-ringed parakeet is a seasonal breeder and is monogamous. This means there is one female that mates with one male. In this species, the female actually attracts the male and initiates the mating. She does this by rubbing her head against the males head repeatedly. After this, the mating process only lasts for a few minutes.

Psittacula krameri is a seasonal breeder that breeds in the winter months of December and January. Rose-ringed parakeets are oviparous, laying eggs in February and March. It is iteroparous, meaning that the bird produces many young each year.

Once the eggs are laid in the nests, the reproductive organs return to a reduced state from April until the next time breeding occurs (December).

Nests are, on average, 640.08 cm off the ground and about 37.8 cm deep. These nests have to be deep enough to hold as many as seven eggs. The rose-ringed parakeet lays on average about four eggs each clutch (range 1-7). Once the eggs are laid, they incubate for about three weeks until the young are hatched.

This species has a high reproductive success, which in turn leads to a high juvenile and adult survival.

Fledging occurs in about seven weeks after hatching. Once these birds reach the age of two years, they are considered to be independent. Males reach sexual maturity at the age of three when they develop the ring around their necks. Female parakeets also reach sexual maturity at the age of three.

The ring-necked parakeet uses a shared roost throughout the year. However, the number of parakeets in the roost during spring decreases dramatically because the female birds stay on the nests while the males return to this roost.

This parakeet is altricial at birth. This means it is fairly underdeveloped and fully dependent on its mother for feeding and protection. Parental care of the young ring-necked parakeets seems to come from both parents.

Once the birds mate, both help with nesting. Both the mother and the father take part in feeding their young and defending their nests until the young birds reach the age of independence.

INDIAN RINGNECK PARAKEET COLORS AND MARKINGS

Ringnecks are available in shades ranging from bright yellows, greens, and blues, to albinos, cinnamons, and lutinos. Though the color mutations are common, the typical coloring of this species is bright lime green with blue tail feathers and yellow under the wings.

They are known as a dimorphic species, meaning that its colors and markings can determine a bird's sex. Males sport deep red beaks, black facial markings, and three bands of color around their necks. The black ring develops at about 18 months, and blue and pink rings appear by the time they reach 3 years old. Females, while still beautiful, lack the facial and collar bands, although some do display a slight darkening of color around their necks.

FEEDING AN INDIAN RINGNECK

Indian Ringnecks are not picky eaters. In fact, almost anything placed into the cage will quickly be devoured. Fresh fruits and vegetables should be placed daily into the cage. It is important these foods be washed and cleaned to avoid pesticides.

A base diet of seeds and pellets should be given to the parrot as well. Using a mixture of conure seed or cockatiel seed will do just fine.

It not a good idea to mix pellets and seeds together as ringnecks will almost often leave the pellets. Instead, they should be rotated weekly to ensure they receive adequate nutrition.

If the ringneck does not eat pellets when introduced, the owner should place them into the cage daily with the seeds to allow time for the parrot to adjust to this new food. Eventually the Indian Ringneck will eat them. Consistency is the key.

If your ringneck is well fed and taken care of, you can expect him to live between 15 to 30 years.

If the ringneck does not eat pellets when introduced, the owner should place them into the cage daily with the seeds to time for the parrot to adjust to this new food. Eventually the Indian Ringneck will eat them. Consistency is the key.

If your ringneck is well fed and taken care of, you can expect him to live between 15 to 30 years.

DIET AND NUTRITION

Wild Indian ringnecks usually feast on a diet of fruits, vegetables, nuts, berries, and seeds. They also enjoy the nectar from flowers and the flowers themselves.

While most vets agree that it is best for captive birds to eat a nutritionally balanced pelleted diet, a ringneck will appreciate a variety of fruits and vegetables in their diet. Leafy greens and vegetables are crucial for any companion parrot to maintain a nutritionally sound diet, and the Indian ringneck parakeet is no exception. They can also eat healthy cooked food you would eat and are particularly fond of chicken, though beans, grains, and rice are also acceptable. Avocados, rhubarb, and chocolate are toxic to birds.

Some ringneck owners find that their bird will sort out and leave behind pellets if it's mixed with seeds. These birds seem picky about eating pellets. If you find that to be the case, offer pellets and seeds separately and rotate them on a regular schedule. They usually come around to pellets. As a rule of thumb, start off by offering your bird 1/4 cup of pellets and 1/4 cup of fruits and vegetables daily. Increase the amount as needed. Remove the uneaten foods to prevent spoilage.

As with all birds, food and water containers should be emptied, cleaned, and refilled daily to reduce the risk of bacterial growth and infection.

In the wild, Ringnecked Parakeets mostly feed on seeds, grains, blossoms, fruits, berries, greens, vegetables, berries, nuts and even nectar.

Flocks of them often forage on farmlands and orchards and are by many farmers considered "crop pests".

They also take advantage of bird feeders in urban gardens.

Especially during the breeding season, the adults and their young have a higher requirement for protein and, therefore, increase their consumption of insects (including beetles), mealworm larvae and pupa.

Captive Diet

Ringnecks should be fed a wide variety of foods. A high quality dry food mix that contains seeds, grains and nuts should be available at all times - a Small Hookbill or Cockatiel should be suitable for them. Clean, fresh water for drinking and bathing should also be provided.

Their diet should also include a good amount of leafy dark greens and vegetables (i.e. chard, kale, carrots, corn, celery, squash), as well as fruits (i.e., applies, grapes, pears, persimmons, pomegranates, figs, grapes, bananas).

Wild-picked green foods such as chickweed, seeding grass, dandelion (flowers, roots and leaves), shepherds-purse and sow-thistle make excellent additions to a healthy diet. Some nutritious human foods, such as cooked beans, cooked chicken, wholegrain rice also add variety to their diet.

Germinated or sprouted seeds are especially important for the breeding season. They should be fed fresh making sure that it is not contaminated by bacteria or molt. It should have a sweet smell. If it smells foul or sour, discard. Frequent rinsing will help prevent spoilage. Sprouting: The Easy Way.

Calcium supplements, such as cuttlefish, shell grit, crushed oyster shell or calcium blocks should be available - particularly during the breeding season.

Millet spray makes a nutritious treat.

WHAT KIND OF PERSONALITY CAN I EXPECT FROM AN INDIAN RINGNECK?

These birds are very active and rarely sit still for more than a few minutes. They can be temperamental and demand a great amount of attention to keep them tame. Lack of interaction with their human companion can cause the bird to become unfriendly and aggressive. Their need for excessive attention makes them unsuitable for first-time bird owners and their potential aggressiveness limits their viability for families with small children.

Indian Ringnecks can be aggressive and territorial, so you should always plan on housing your birds in their own sleeping cage. They can get along very well with others of their kind if given enough space. If considering other species make sure that they are sized appropriately.

Strong bonds will be formed with their human companion by these birds, with the females generally forming stronger bonds. They love to ride around on their human's shoulder as much as possible. Socializing with all family members is a good practice to limit jealousy issues.

A distinctive behavior engaged in by the Indian Ringneck is the practice called bluffing. After weaning your bird will encounter this phase, which may last from a few weeks to several months. It is a period of increased aggression during which the owner should avoid having the bird on their shoulder.

These intelligent birds can learn to talk and perform tricks. The best results will be achieved through positive reinforcement and gentle dominance exhibited by their human caretakers. They will attempt to take advantage of you if you let them, so be cautious not to allow any unwanted behaviors like biting to become a problem.

FEMALE SPECIFIC BEHAVIORS

Female Indian ringneck parakeets are angry, boisterous birds that will kill their mate if the female decides she dislikes him. Supervision must be constant with birds that are not constantly caged together due to this predatory, territorial instinct in female birds. Female ringnecks that are ready for breeding will crouch and tilt their heads back to entice males caged near them. When the male is introduced, even interested females can decide to chase the male around the cage and torment him for a short period of time. If the female does not calm down, try moving the pair to a cage neither of them has been in before.

MALE SPECIFIC BEHAVIORS

During the breeding season, sexually mature males will be ready to mate with any willing female. Bowing and staring at female birds caged near him are two steady signs that a male wants to breed with a particular female. If the female and male are kept together year-round, the pair will become far more affectionate with one another. This includes grooming each other, nestling on the same perch and making noises much like cooing.

CARING FOR YOUR INDIAN RINGNECK

A wide range of temperatures is tolerated by these hardy birds as evidenced by the wide distribution of feral populations. As they are very active, you should opt for the largest cage you can provide, as well as plenty of time outside the cage. The minimum cage size for a single Indian Ringneck is 24Lx24Wx36H inches (61×61.91.5 cm) with 1/2 to 5/8 inch (1.27 to 1.58 cm) bar spacing.

Cages should be well stocked with interesting toys and chewable objects to keep your birds from becoming bored. Your bird's intelligence demands adequate mental stimulation when you cannot give your direct attention.

The bird's diet should consist of pellets, seeds and fresh fruit and vegetables. It may take some effort to get your bird to accept the pellets, but it is worth it when considering the bird's health.

Molting is a yearly process and starts when the bird reaches approximately six months of age. Your bird may become a bit grumpy at this time. They love baths and should get the opportunity as often as possible. Nail trimming may occasionally be necessary but can be minimized by employing some concrete perches.

Breeding is legal and can be done in two ways, One method houses the paired birds permanently while the other method keeps the genders separate until it is time to breed.

CAGES FOR RINGNECK PARAKEETS

Ringneck parakeets should be kept in the largest cage that you can accommodate. At a bare minimum a large cockatiel cage should be considered. Better yet, long cages measuring some four to six feet in length are recommended, with perches placed at either end. In such a cage your Ringneck will be able to exercise their powers of flight, as well as climbing and crawling around their cage.

Note that like all caged birds, ringnecks can be messy feeders. It is not unusual to find a cage surrounded by bird sand, grit, feathers and shucked food. Owners should be ready to either vacuum around their pets cage on a regular basis, or to place the cage where minimal damage will be done.

While Ringneck Parakeets can survive a cold British winter snuggled up with friends, particularly damp, cold or windy weather is best avoided. When deciding where to place your cage try placing it away from potential sources of drafts – such as external doors or windows. Also avoid the risk of overheating, by ensuring that direct sunlight in the summer months cannot cook your bird alive.

If you have the budget to house your parakeets in an aviary then all the better. The extra space and environmental enrichment that these surroundings offer are greatly appreciated. All the same, ensure that your parakeet has someone dry and secure to hide away from the worst of the weather. A weather-proofed roosting area tends to work well.

FUN FACTS ABOUT INDIAN RINGNECK

Indian ringneck parakeets are quite popular companion birds, thanks in part to their beautiful coloring, medium size, and social nature. These birds are highly intelligent and enjoy learning new things. But they do require an attentive caretaker who can spend time handling them every day to keep them tame and prevent them from becoming bored. If you're interested in bringing home one of these birds, first learn about some of the fascinating traits Indian ringneck parakeets possess.

Indian Ringneck Parakeets Defy Their 'Difficult' Reputation

Indian ringneck parakeets have been kept in captivity for centuries but were regarded as an "ornamental," or hands-off, bird species. Ringnecks still have a reputation of being somewhat nippy and difficult to tame. However, those who have grown to know these birds have found they can make loving pets when hand-fed as babies and properly socialized.

Ringnecks that are handled every day by their caretakers generally have charming personalities. They love working on new bird tricks, such as waving hello with a foot, with their humans. And they enjoy other mental challenges, including figuring out treat puzzles and learning to mimic sounds.

Ringnecks Might Cause Some Trouble During Adolescence

While ringnecks overall don't deserve their "difficult" reputation, they can be a handful during their adolescence. Like some other bird species, young ringnecks—usually those between 4 months and 1 year old—often go through what's called a "bluffing" phase. During this phase, hormonal changes can increase a bird's aggressive tendencies, such as hissing, biting, and general resistance to interaction.

Some inexperienced owners might make the mistake of avoiding interacting with their bird during this phase, which can make the bird even more antisocial. The key to getting through the bluffing phase is to keep trying to bond with your bird while encouraging good behaviors. And remember that the phase should be over in less than a few months.

Ringnecks Are Referred to as Parrots and Parakeets

Although identified as a parakeet, Indian ringnecks (like all parakeets) are also parrots. These birds have been labeled as parakeets because of their medium size and long tail feathers—trademark features of all parakeets. Still, many people refer to them as Indian ringneck parrots, which is also accurate.

Despite its medium size, the bird's long parakeet tail causes it to need a larger cage than one might think. However, make sure the bar spacing of a large cage isn't wide enough that the bird can get stuck or escape between bars. In addition, this active species needs lots of space outside of the cage to stretch its wings and play.

They Come in a Variety of Colors

Wild Indian ringneck parakeets are normally mostly bright green with some blue tail feathers and yellow under their wings. Male ringnecks sport black and rose rings around their necks, as well as black facial markings.

However, selective breeding programs have given rise to a number of beautiful color mutations within the species. This has led to ringnecks whose dominant color is blue, yellow, or white, among other striking color combinations. In many places, the color-mutated birds have become even more popular than the green ringnecks.

Indian Ringneck Parakeets Are Excellent Talkers

While it's never a sure thing that your bird will be able to learn to talk, opting to adopt an Indian ringneck parakeet will certainly up your chances. These birds are notorious talkers. In fact, they were once considered sacred in their native environment based on their remarkable ability to mimic human speech. Long ago, religious leaders in India observed the birds repeating prayers that were recited daily in the gardens surrounding their places of worship.

The clarity of their speech, along with their ability to learn dozens (if not hundreds) of words, still continues to surprise people. Ringneck voices are one of the most charming among companion birds, as they tend to be comically high-pitched. They typically start talking between 8 months and 1 year old and are quick learners, especially if their humans spend quality time talking to them every day.

WHERE TO ADOPT OR BUY AN INDIAN RINGNECK PARAKEET

Indian ringnecks are relatively common in the United States and can be rescued, adopted, or purchased at verified organizations like RescueParrots.org or adoption websites like Petfinder. Pricing ranges from $400 to $500, though you can expect to pay up to $700 depending on the organization and the bird.

If you're going the breeder route, make sure that the breeder is reputable by asking them how long they've been breeding and working with Indian ringneck parakeets. Ask for a tour, but don't be alarmed if you are unable to tour the facilities in which they keep the birds. Many reputable breeders opt to work under closed aviaries, which prevents diseases from infecting the flock.

Also, make sure that the bird you want to take home is as healthy. Make sure the parakeet is alert, active, and exhibits all the signs of a healthy bird, such as bright eyes, clean feathers, and full crops.

CONCLUSION

Indian ringnecks are some of the most widely-distributed parrots found anywhere on earth. Their natural habitat stretches from arid western Africa right through to the humid monsoon forests of India. As you might expect, the Indian Ringneck is an astonishingly adaptable bird, capable of surviving in all manner of habitats.

It should be little wonder that the Indian Ringneck has subsequently become an alien resident in many other parts of the world thanks to the pet trade and the natural ability of escapees to thrive under almost any circumstances. The RSPB, for example, claim there are over 8,000 pairs living and breeding in the United Kingdom, where dozens of birds roost in groups around London and outlying counties.

This same adaptability, and the intelligence that leads to it, can make the Indian Ringneck parakeet a fascinating pet for owners of all ages.

Indian Ringnecks are rather misunderstood birds in many ways. Any negative press directed at them is really just an extension of their intelligence, and ability to cope under a wide variety of conditions. With patience, and the right level of care, Indian ringneck parakeets can become long-lived, confiding and highly entertaining pets for all the family.

Just be sure to do your research thoroughly before bringing home your new parakeets as they represent a long-term commitment.